FAMOUS AIR FORCE BOMBERS

12599

GEORGE SULLIVAN

DODD, MEAD & COMPANY
New York

1   2   3   4   5   6   7   8   9   10

Library of Congress Cataloging in Publication Data

Sullivan, George, 1927-
  Famous air force bombers.

  Summary: A history of the bombers used by the Air
Force through the years with descriptions of the various
kinds.
  1. Bombers—United States—Juvenile literature.
2. Aeronautics, Military—United States—History—
Juvenile literature.   3. United States.   Air Force—
History—Juvenile literature.   [1. Bombers.   2. Airplanes.
3. Aeronautics, Military—History.   4. United States.
Air Force—History]   I. Title.
UG1242.B6S85   1985   358.4'2'0973   85-6973
ISBN 0-396-08621-7

INTRODUCTION

Military aviation began soon after the first successful balloon ascent in France in 1782 and the first manned balloon crossing of the English Channel two years later.

The French government, realizing the military importance of these two events, sent up soldiers in balloons to observe enemy troop movements. That was in 1794.

In this country, experience with balloons during the Civil War showed that they were useful for making aerial observations and directing gunfire by means of telegraphic communication with the ground.

Aviation took a great leap forward in 1903 when the Wright Brothers made the first power-driven airplane flight.

Four years later, the U.S. Army Signal Corps established an Aeronautical Division with the responsibility of developing military balloons and flying machines.

In these early times, planes did not play different roles. There were no "fighters," as such, no "bombers."

Bombers and fighters began to develop as distinct types of planes during World War I, which raged in Europe from 1914 to 1918.

During the war and for years afterward, military planners stressed the development of fighter planes. Bomber projects moved slowly.

But when new engines were developed in the late 1920s and early 1930s that produced more horsepower for less weight, bomber speed and range increased. And so did the importance of the plane.

American and British bombers played a vital role in smashing Hitler's Europe and winning World War II. The fame of some World War II bombers—chiefly the B-17 Flying Fortress and B-29 Superfortress—has lasted to this day.

After the war, jet-powered bombers became the standard. The Korean War and the war in Vietnam triggered more advances in the speed, range, and sophistication of all military aircraft.

The pages that follow profile the aircraft that have had the greatest influence on bomber development, from the time of the Wright Brothers to the present day. There's also a glimpse of the "ghost" bombers of tomorrow, aircraft that will be able to evade electronic detection by the enemy.

The aircraft described and pictured in this book appear in the approximate order each was introduced.

The author is grateful to many individuals who helped him in the preparation of this book. Special thanks are due Maj. William H. Austin and Capt. Peter S. Meltzer, Air Force Office of Public Affairs, Arlington, Virginia; Robert Waller and Tom Cross, Defense Audio-Video Agency, Washington, D.C.; Dana Bell, National Air and Space Museum, Washington, D.C.; Z. Joe Thornton and J. F. Isabel, General Dynamics; Harold Carr, Marilyn A. Phipps, and Jack Wecker, The Boeing Company; Ira E. Chart and Peggy Nuovo, The Northrop Corporation; Robert C. Ferguson, Lockheed-California Company; Francene Crum, Martin Marietta Corp.; Sylvia Brown, De Havilland Aircraft of Canada, Ltd.; Francesca Kurti, TLC Custom Labs; Herb Field, Herb Field Studios; Bill Sullivan and Leon Greene.

CONTENTS

Wright plane is towed to parade ground at Fort Myer for testing.

WRIGHT MILTARY FLYER

On December 23, 1907, the Signal Corps of the U.S. Army issued specifications covering the construction of a "heavier-than-air flying machine" that would be the first military aircraft.

They read:

• The flying machine should be designed to carry two persons having a combined weight of 350 pounds, also sufficient fuel for a flight of 125 miles.

• The machine should be designed to have a speed of 40 miles per hour in still air.

• It . . . should be designed so that it may be quickly and easily assembled and taken apart and packed for transportation in army wagons.

No fewer than forty-one proposals were received by the Signal Corps. Bids ranged from a low of $500 to a high of $1 million.

The proposal that was finally accepted came from the Wright Brothers, who had invented the airplane four years before. They said they could provide the plane the Signal Corps wanted for $25,000.

The Wrights built a wire-braced biplane with a Wright 25-hp, four-cylinder engine driven by two wooden propellers. Its wooden framework wings and control surfaces were covered with fabric. It had wooden skids to serve as a landing gear.

They began testing the plane, which they called the "Flyer," at Fort Myer, Virginia, on September 3, 1908, when Orville got it into the air and remained aloft for one minute, eleven seconds. Several days of even more successful test-flying followed.

But two weeks later, tragedy struck. Orville, carrying Lt. Thomas Selfridge as a passenger, was making a routine turn when the propeller struck a brace wire and shattered. The plane, then at 150 feet, glided gently to about 75 feet, but then plunged like a stone to the ground. Orville suffered several injuries, including a broken hip. Lieutenant Selfridge was killed, the first fatality in military aviation.

During the summer of the following year, the Wrights returned to Fort Myer with an improved machine, and spent several weeks testing it. On July 27, 1909, Orville flew with Lt. Frank P. Lahm for 1 hour, 12 minutes, thus fulfilling a Signal Corps requirement that the plane remain aloft at least one hour with a passenger. The plane covered about forty miles during the flight. On August 2, 1909, the Signal Corps accepted its first flying machine.

Wright Military Flyer during Fort Myer tests

Other Data (Model: Wright Type A)
Wingspan: 36 ft., 6 in.
Length: 28 ft., 11 in.
Power Plant: One 30-hp Wright
Loaded Weight: 735 lb.
Maximum Speed: 40 mph

Despite some shortcomings, the DH-4 performed many useful missions during World War I.

DE HAVILLAND DH-4

When World War I was declared in 1914, European aircraft designers and builders began to produce several different types of bombing "machines." The United States, however, lagged behind in aircraft development.

A U.S. Commission was sent to Europe to study the aircraft being produced. The Commission recommended that Americans begin building two highly regarded aircraft—the French Spad pursuit plane and the De Havilland DH-4 bombing plane.

Just as work was about to begin on the Spad, it was decided to let the French build pursuit planes, and plans for their production in America were cancelled. American manufacturers were assigned to concentrate on making a bomber, the De Havilland DH-4.

Eventually, 4,846 DH-4s were built. Of these, 1,213 reached France and 543 flew in combat.

Many of the DH-4s delivered to American pilots were so lacking in workmanship that they were unfit to fly. Even when put together properly, the DH-4 was a clumsy plane, as unforgiving at the controls as an overloaded truck.

Worse, a large and fragile fuel tank was located just behind the pilot's seat. The tank could be exploded by a single incendiary bullet. The DH-4 was quickly given the nickname of "Flying Coffin."

Despite is shortcomings, the DH-4 performed many worthwhile missions. On October 9, 1918, during the Meuse-Argonne offensive, Gen. William "Billy" Mitchell ordered more than 350 bombers and fighters to attack German troops who were preparing to counterattack American forces. The DH-4s played an important role in the raid, the heaviest air attack of the war. Some 32 tons of bombs were dumped on the enemy. The Germans were so stunned they called off their counteroffensive.

After World War I, DH-4s were used to pioneer many of the airmail routes in the United States. Some planes remained in service until as late as 1932.

Other Data (Model: DH-4)
Wingspan: 42 ft., 6 in.
Length: 29 ft., 11 in.
Power Plant: One 420-hp Liberty
Loaded Weight: 4,297 lb.
Maximum Speed: 124 mph

After World War I, D-H 4 played an important role in developing U.S. air mail routes.

Its two 400-hp Liberty engines gave the MB-2 a cruising speed in excess of 100 mph.

MARTIN MB-1, MB-2

The United States, in spite of being the birthplace of manned flight, failed to produce a single combat-worthy airplane during World War I.

The thousands of American pilots who were sent to Europe during the war were forced to fly the somewhat popular but unreliable Spads, old Nieuport fighters, which French pilots didn't want to fly, or the British-designed and American-built De Havilland DH-4s, which were even more accident-prone than the Nieuports.

In an effort to correct this situation, the infant Glenn L. Martin Company was asked to design a plane that would outperform Britain's big Handley-Page 0/400, the world's first strategic bomber. A young designer named Donald Douglas was put in charge of the project.

Douglas drew up plans for the MB-1, which was not as big as the Handley-Page, but had a higher speed. The Aircraft Production Board in Washington, D.C., was so impressed with the

MB-1, it ordered ten of them. The first of these was test-flown on August 17, 1918.

World War I ended before the MB-1 saw service, and production was halted. But Douglas designed an improved version of the plane, the MB-2.

The MB-2 earned big headlines in 1921 when Brig. Gen. William "Billy" Mitchell used the plane to prove his belief that airplanes could sink and destroy any Navy ship in existence. In one test, MB-2s, loaded with 600-pound bombs, sent the German cruiser *Frankfort* to the bottom within thirty-five minutes.

A sterner challenge was presented by the German battleship *Ostfriesland*, a 27,000-ton, battle-tough veteran. Navy officials said the *Ostfriesland* was unsinkable.

Shortly before noon on July 21, 1921, six MB-2s and two Handley-Page 0/400s, each plane carrying a 2,000-pound bomb, took off from Langley Field, Virginia. The *Ostfriesland* was anchored off the Virginia coast. A bomb in the water close to the vessel lifted the battleship into the air, and a direct hit split the ship and sent clouds of smoke billowing into the sky. After another bomb struck close to the ship's stern, the *Ostfriesland* turned over. A final bomb sent the ship to the bottom. It had taken less than twenty-two minutes. The doctrine of airpower as a military weapon had never been more clearly demonstrated.

An **MB-2,** the first **U.S.-designed strategic bomber,** cruises over nation's capital.

Other Data (Model: MB-2)
Wingspan: 71 ft., 5 in.
Length: 46 ft., 4 in.
Power Plant: Two 400-hp liquid-cooled Liberties
Loaded Weight: 12,075 lb.
Maximum Speed: 107 mph

Curtiss Condors at March Field, California, in 1934

CURTISS B-2 CONDOR

Bombing planes of the early to mid-1920s showed little improvement over the MB-2, the ship with which Brig. Gen Billy Mitchell made headlines. Most bombers were underpowered, could carry only small bomb loads, and were limited as to how high they could fly.

The best of the lot was the Curtiss Condor, built in 1924. A biplane powered with two 600-hp engines, and with a top speed of 132 miles an hour, it remained a first-line aircraft until the 1930s. It has been called America's first strategic bomber.

Aluminum tubing was used for the Condor's fuselage and wing ribs. Steel spars in the wings and steel tubing in the bomb bay provided added strength. The fuselage and wings were covered in the traditional manner, with fabric.

One unusual innovation was an exposed turret behind the housing of each of the plane's two engines. A twin .30-caliber machine gun on a swivel was mounted in each turret. These, plus twin .30s in the nose, endowed the Condor with more firepower than any other bomber of the time.

The tactical mission of the Condor was to provide maximum support for ground forces. Thus, enemy troops and equipment were deemed the plane's chief targets, meaning the bomber of this period played a role similar to that of today's attack and close-support aircraft.

Air power theories of the 1920s assumed that planes would attack in daylight. Pursuit planes would first have to sweep the skies clear of enemy aircraft to permit the bombers' safe flight. Formation flying was established as another means of mutual defense.

While the superior qualities of the Condor were well known, the plane was never ordered in great quantities by the Air Corps because it was too costly. Instead, funds that had been appropriated were used to buy a bomber produced by the Keystone Aviation Corporation. The Keystone was not quite as good a plane as the Condor, but it had the advantage of being less expensive.

In total, only twelve Condors were purchased by the Air Corps. The first was delivered in 1929. Condors remained in service until the mid-1930s, the last until 1936.

Other Data (Model: B-2)
Wingspan: 90 ft.
Length: 47 ft., 6 in.
Power Plant: Two 600-hp Curtiss Conquerers
Loaded Weight: 16,516 lb.
Maximum Speed: 132 mph

A quartet of Condors during simulated long-distance bombing raid above California's Death Valley

A squadron of Keystone bombers fly in formation near Langley Field, Virginia.

KEYSTONE

Virtually all of the bombing techniques used by the Air Force during World War II in the 1940s were based on training and maneuvers conducted during the late 1920s and early 1930s by the two organizations that preceded the U.S. Air Force—the Air Service and the Army Air Corps. (The name was changed to Army Air Force in 1941.)

Bombing tests were sometimes directed against obsolete Air Corps fighters and light bombers, principally DH-4s, which were lined up in neat rows. Plane after plane would then be reduced to wreckage.

Such maneuvers also involved bridge-busting, smashing concrete, steel, or wooden spans upon which the enemy forces depended for supply and reinforcement.

As early as 1927 the Air Corps was practicing bridge-busting. In one test, the target was North Carolina's Pee Dee River bridge, which the Army Engineers had been ordered to destroy. Twin-engine bombers—Keystones—from Pope Field near Fort Bragg, North Carolina, did the job.

The Keystones attacked one by one or in formation, at different altitudes, and with bombs of assorted sizes. The lessons learned from these simulated air strikes influenced bombing strategy for decades.

The Keystone Aviation Corporation produced several different models of its bomber, all of which were basically the same except for engine modifications. All versions had a crew of five—a pilot, copilot, bombardier, and two gunners.

Some models had three .30-caliber machine guns, while others had five guns. The bomb load ranged from 2,000 to 2,500 pounds. The plane's fuselage as well as the wings were fabric-covered.

Slightly more than 150 Keystones were ordered by the Air Corps, making it the No. 1 bomber of its time. But the fact that most pursuit planes of the day could fly rings around the Keystone and other bombers led most military leaders to concentrate on fighter plane development. Despite their achievements in destroying "enemy" aircraft and bridge-busting, this was not a golden period for the bomber.

Other Data (Model: B-6A)
Wingspan: 74 ft., 9 in.
Length: 48 ft., 10 in.
Power Plant: Two 575-hp Pratt & Whitney Hornets
Loaded Weight: 13,474 pounds
Maximum Speed: 121 mph

Keystone bomber carried a crew of five—a pilot, copilot, bombardier, and two gunners.

CURTISS A-12 SHRIKE

While the Curtiss A-12 Shrike was not especially fast and had limited bomb-carrying ability, it earned a place in aviation history. It was the first all-metal, low-wing monoplane to see service with the Air Corps, the first with an enclosed cockpit, and the first with wing flaps to reduce landing speed.

The Air Corps had seen the need for a plane such as the Shrike as early as 1930, the year it ordered its first low-wing, all-metal attack bomber. General Aviation responded with the XA-7, while Curtiss countered with the XA-8. In flight tests conducted during 1931, the Curtiss plane outflew its rival. The Air Corps then ordered thirteen of them.

After two engine changes, both of which were meant to increase the plane's power, the designation was revised to A-10. Additional improvements, including the substitution of a Wright Cyclone engine, resulted in the A-12.

The Shrike was fitted out with four forward-firing machine guns, plus one swivel gun in the rear cockpit.

In its wing racks and below the fuselage, the Shrike could carry 400 pounds of bombs. The plane could also tote extra fuel in a tank beneath the fuselage.

Formation of A-12s over the Hawaiian Islands in 1938

16

A Curtiss A-12 Shrike releases a parachute bomb during test run.

The Air Corps was never entirely happy with the Shrike, and only about sixty of them were ordered. All the while, the Air Corps was pressing for new aircraft designs that would offer greater speed and more bomb-carrying capability. These demands were to be answered in the form of the B-9, B-10 and, eventually, the B-17.

Other Data (Model: A-12)
Wingspan: 44 ft.
Length: 32 ft., 3 in.
Power Plant: One 690-hp Wright Cyclone
Loaded Weight: 5,745 lb.
Maximum Speed: 177 mph at sea level

BOEING B-9 DEATH ANGEL

During the early 1930s, two advances in airplane manufacture revolutionized bomber development. These were single-wing, or monoplane, design and all-metal construction. Both of these advances were featured in the Boeing B-9, an experimental version which was first flown on April 29, 1931.

Before the introduction of the B-9, all large aircraft of monoplane construction had their engines mounted either above or below the wings. Boeing engineers thought there might be a better way. After consulting with the National Advisory Committee for Aeronautics and conducting tests with model planes, it was decided to mount the engines in front of the wings.

The airplane was judged a triumph from the first day it was flown. Other advances it featured included air-cooled engines and a retractable landing gear, the first ever on a military airplane.

Able to achieve a speed of 188 mph, the B-9 was faster than any other bomber of the time. It was also faster than many fighter planes.

One failing the B-9 had was that it could carry a bombload of only 900 pounds, less than half that of the World War I Handley-Page 0/400. That didn't seem to bother the Air Corps, however.

It purchased the first test model, designating it

With a cruising speed of 188 mph, the B-9 was faster than most fighter planes of the day.

First flown in 1931, the B-9 ushered in an era of all-metal, single-wing bombers.

the XB-901. On the flight from the Boeing factory in Seattle, Washington, to Wright Field in Dayton, Ohio, the plane averaged a surprising 155 mph, and only two refueling stops were required.

Before the B-9, the standard Air Corps bombers were the Keystone B-3 and the Curtiss Condor, both of which had fabric-covered wings, a design feature that hearkened back to the Wright Brothers. The all-metal B-9 was a great leap forward.

Nevertheless, the B-9 never went into large-scale production. A still faster bomber, and one that boasted gun-turret bubbles, had been developed by the Martin Company. Known as the B-10, it was ordered into mass production by the Air Corps in preference to the B-9.

Other Data (Model Y1B-9A)
Wingspan: 76 ft., 9 in.
Length: 51 ft., 5 in.
Power Plant: Two 630-hp air-cooled Pratt & Whitney Hornets
Loaded Weight: 13,919 lb.
Maximum Speed: 188 mph at 6,000 ft.

With a cruising speed in excess of 200 mph and a range of 600 mph, the B-10 overshadowed all other bombers of its time.

A lineup of B-10Bs at Langley Field, Virginia, before a bombing demonstration

MARTIN B-10 FLYING WHALE

After the Martin B-10 made its first test flight on March 10, 1932, Air Corps generals clapped their hands. The B-10, at 207 mph, was faster than any other bomber of the day, including the B-9, and even faster than most fighters then in service.

The five-man crew rode in enclosed cockpits and gun-turret bubbles. (It was the first U.S. bomber to be fitted with a gun turret.) The plane had a range of 600 miles. While its bombload was only 600 pounds, the B-10 seemed to be the perfect tactical model then needed to assist in Army ground operations.

The B-10 was ordered into mass production. To demonstrate the plane's reliability, Lt. Col. Hap Arnold led a squadron of the bombers on a mass flight from Washington, D.C., to Alaska. Ten bombers started and, following a 7,360-mile round trip, ten returned. During the journey, more than 20,000 square miles of Alaska was photographed as an aid in mapping.

Through the years, the Air Corps had a good deal of success in selling B-10s to foreign governments. The Flying Whale was operated by the air forces of Argentina, China, the Netherlands, Philippines, and Turkey.

The Martin B-10 remained in service with the U.S. Air Corps until the late 1930s, when it was replaced by Boeing B-17s and Douglas B-18s.

A Martin B-10 in flight over Panama

B-10s operated by Dutch crews in the Netherlands East Indies were among the first U.S.-built planes flown in combat in World War II. In one mission, twelve B-10s sank twenty-six enemy vessels, including a battleship.

Other Data (Model: B-10B)
Wingspan: 70 ft., 6 in.
Length: 44 ft., 9 in.
Power Plant: Two 700-hp air-cooled Wright
    Cyclones
Loaded Weight: 14,887 pounds
Maximum Speed: 215 mph

The B-17 featured such innovations as a retractable landing gear and fully enclosed bomb bay.

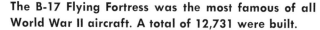

The B-17 Flying Fortress was the most famous of all World War II aircraft. A total of 12,731 were built.

BOEING B-17 FLYING FORTRESS

If there is one airplane that can be said to symbolize Allied air superiority during World War II, that plane is the B-17 Flying Fortress, the first all-metal, four-engine, single-wing bomber. It could fly long distances at extreme heights, carrying up to eight tons of bombs, had gun blisters or turrets "everywhere you looked," and was a dream to fly.

The B-17 had only one failing: its scarcity. At the time of Pearl Harbor, the Air Force had only 117 B-17s. But by the end of the war, 12,731 B-17s had been built—6,981 by Boeing, 2,750 by Lockheed, and 3,000 by Douglas. It ranked as the most famous of all World War II aircraft.

The B-17 was called Model 299 when first tested on July 28, 1935. The plane boasted such innovations as a tail wheel, retractable landing gear, and fully enclosed bomb bay with electrically operated bay doors. A newspaperman who covered the roll-out ceremony called it a "flying fortress"—and the name stuck.

On August 20, 1935, a model 299 prototype completed a long-distance flight from Seattle, Washington, to Dayton, Ohio, a distance of 2,100 miles, in slightly over nine hours, averaging a speed of 233 mph, a tremendous achievement for the day.

Although the prototype later crashed when the pilot took off with the rudder and elevators in a locked position, the Air Force placed an order for thirteen B-17s. The first production model was delivered to Langley Field, Virginia, on March 1, 1937.

The Air Force ordered 39 B-17s and 38 B-17Cs in 1939. These planes were delivered in 1940. They differed from the earlier models by having more powerful engines and seven machines guns, not merely five.

In the years that followed, the B-17 went through one design change after another. The B-17E, introduced in September, 1941, was more heavily armed than earlier models. Since experience had shown the huge plane to be nearly defenseless when attacked from the rear, a tail gun position was added that housed a pair of .50-caliber machine guns.

The B-17G had an additional gun turret beneath the plane's nose. It was called a "chin" turret.

The B-17G, flown for the first time in May, 1943, featured an additional gun turret beneath the plane's nose, a "chin" turret, as it was called. Waist gunners in B-17Gs were provided 600 rounds of ammunition per gun, twice the amount of those on B-17Fs. The new Flying Fortresses could stay aloft for almost nine hours and they had a range of 1,850 miles. Nearly 9,000 B-17Gs were built, more than any other model.

The B-17 won its greatest fame in Europe. On the afternoon of August 17, 1942, twelve Flying

B-17s roll off the Boeing Company's assembly line.

Fortresses of the Eighth Bomber Command attacked the railroad yards at Rouen, France. That raid launched the Air Force's heavy bomber offensive against Germany.

With at least half of the bombs falling from an altitude of 23,000 feet into one target area, the raid, according to an official report, "far exceeded in accuracy any previous high-altitude bombing in the European Theater of operations by German or Allied Aircraft."

There was little antiaircraft fire. German fighters were easily fended off by the heavily armed planes. The only casualites were two crewmen who suffered cuts from flying plexiglass when a bird shattered the airplane's nose on the return flight.

In time, the U.S. Eighth Air Force in England became so strong that it was able to send more than a thousand Flying Fortresses on a single mission. The German Air Force defended its nation grimly, and Allied losses increased steadily as the enemy threw more and more of its strength into bomber defense. A year after the first raid against Rouen, the Eighth Air Force lost 59 bombers over Schweinfurt and Regensburg—more than the Americans lost in the first six months of bombing.

American B-17s hit oil refineries and aircraft and

chemical industries, motor vehicle and synthetic-rubber plants. They struck at air bases and shipyards. They supported ground troops and dropped propaganda leaflets. Some were fitted out for use in air-sea rescue work, photoreconnaissance, and for cargo or passenger transport.

They were not only widely used in Europe and the Middle East, but also saw service in every other area of the world where U.S. forces saw action. In the Pacific theater of operations, they were used for both tactical and close-support bombing and also saw reconnaissance duty.

The B-17 continued in use for more than a decade after World War II, although its numbers sharply dwindled. Israel, in the 1948 war against surrounding Arab states, used three B-17s in conducting bombing raids. In the Korean War, which erupted in 1950, the first missions over North Korea were flown by a B-17 fitted out for aerial mapping. And much later, when the conflict in Vietnam was beginning to heat up, a B-17 was used in parachuting CIA agents into the country.

Other Data (Model: B-17G)
Wingspan: 103 ft., 9 in.
Length: 74 ft., 4 in.
Power Plant: Four 1,200-hp air-cooled Wright
    Cyclones
Loaded Weight: 65,500
Maximum Speed: 287 mph at 25,000 ft.

B-17E, introduced in 1941, was first with a tail gun position that housed a pair of .50-caliber machine guns.

Although sturdy and dependable, the B-18 Digby lacked in speed and range.

DOUGLAS B-18 DIGBY

On September 3, 1939, when Adolph Hitler unleashed the ground and air attack against Poland that was to trigger World War II, the standard U.S. Army Air Corps bomber was the Douglas B-18 Digby, a military version of the company's successful DC-2 commercial airliner. A twin-engine medium bomber, the B-18 soon won a reputation for being a sturdy and dependable ship.

The B-18, being larger than the Martin B-10 and capable of carrying a heavier payload, was a big improvement over the earlier plane. Not long after the plane was test-flown at Wright Field in Dayton, Ohio, in September, 1935, the Air Corps ordered 133 B-18s.

Even so, Air Corps officials were not entirely happy with the B-18. They wanted something more than sturdiness and dependability. The B-18's maximum speed was a mere 215 mph and its range was sorely limited.

During the mid-to-late 1930s, Douglas worked to improve the plane. The engine was beefed up to give additional horsepower and structural changes were made in the fuselage and wing, boosting the plane's airspeed to 282 mph.

An additional 177 B-18s were ordered by the Air Corps in 1937. Production eventually reached 350. All versions of the aircraft had three gun positions, each a .30-caliber machine gun.

Despite these improvements, the Air Corps would have preferred to have a four-engine bomber, a plane capable of carrying several tons of bombs at good speed over long range. These wishes were realized with the B-17 Flying Fortress, which was eventually ordered by the thousands. Production of the B-18 was abandoned.

Most of the Army Air Corps' bomber squadrons were equipped with B-18As in 1940. Thirty-three were sitting ducks for Japanese bombers at Hickam

A formation of B-18As over Miami, Florida, in 1940

Field, Hawaii, on December 7, 1941, when Pearl Harbor was attacked.

Beginning in 1942, B-18s in frontline service were replaced by B-17s. But the B-18s were not retired. Some 122 of them were fitted out with radar and MAD (magnetic anomaly detection) gear and began toiling in the Caribbean area as submarine patrol craft. The Royal Canadian Air Force acquired twenty B-18s for the same use. Many other B-18s saw service as transports or were used in pilot training. But the B-18 never fulfilled the mission for which it had been designed and built.

Other Data (Model: B-18A)
Wingspan: 89 ft., 6 in.
Length: 57 ft., 10 in.
Power Plant. Two 1,000-hp Wright Cyclones
Loaded Weight: 22,675 lb.
Maxium Speed: 215 mph at 10,000 ft.

More B-24 Liberators were built and used during World War II than any other aircraft.

CONSOLIDATED B-24 LIBERATOR

Like the B-17 Flying Fortress, the four-engine B-24 Liberator was a workhorse bomber of World War II. More B-24s were built and used during the war than any other airplane, a total of 19,251 in all versions.

Many pilots of the day argued that the B-24 was a better plane than the B-17. There was plenty of evidence to support that claim. It boasted a faster rate of climb than the B-17, longer range, and the ability to carry a bigger load of explosives. While the B-17's maximum speed was greater than that of the B-24, the Liberator had a higher cruising speed.

Pilots also liked the plane because it was a veritable flying battleship, with guns everywhere. There were waist guns, nose guns, tail guns, and gun turrets on top of the fuselage and in the belly.

The Liberator's beginnings date to January, 1939, when Air Corps officials asked Consolidated to design a bomber with performance characteristics superior to those of the B-17, which was starting to roll off production lines. Consolidated had already begun work on such a plane. The first plans and specifications were ready in a matter of weeks. Flight-testing of the first model began late in 1939.

On January 27, 1943, Liberators (along with B-17s) took part in the first penetration of German air space by American bombers when they attacked the submarine pens at Wilhelmshaven. Some one hundred German fighters attacked the 91-plane formation.

B-24s took part in one of the most famous bombing raids of World War II, the low-level attack upon the Ploesti petroleum refineries in Romania. The mission was launched on August 1, 1943, when 178 B-24s, loaded to capacity, took off from Benghazi in Libya for the 1,350-mile flight across the Mediterranean to Ploesti. German radar picked up the planes as they drew near, and enemy fighter planes were waiting. Haystacks in the fields on the approach to the refineries turned out to be hidden antiaircraft nests. Planes were shot to pieces by flak. Fifty-four Liberators failed to return from the mission.

But Ploesti was an exception. In Europe, the Pacific, and in the skies over Japan in the war's final stages, the Liberator scored more victories over enemy aircraft than any other type of bomber in service with the Allies.

Other Data (Model: B-24J)
Wingspan: 100 ft.
Length: 67 ft., 3 in.
Power Plant: For 1,200-hp air-cooled Pratt
 & Whitney Twin Wasps
Loaded Weight: 60,000 lb.
Maximum Speed: 294 mph at 32,000 ft.

A lineup of B-24s at Tinker Field, Oklahoma City, Oklahoma

Douglas A-20 Havocs were among the first bombers to see action in World War II.

DOUGLAS A-20 HAVOC

Even before the onset of World War II and the production activity that made the United States No. 1 in the air, the Army Air Corps enjoyed worldwide superiority in light and medium two-engine bombers, this thanks to three planes—the Douglas A-20 Havoc, the North American B-25 Mitchell, and the Martin B-26 Marauder. All three were available in some quantity before the attack on Pearl Harbor and went on to serve with distinction in every theater of the war.

The A-20 Havoc, designed by Douglas Aircraft in 1936, was first ordered by the French government. Planes began to be delivered to French forces in August, 1939.

When Germany knocked France out of the war in May, 1940, the British took over the A-20 contract. The U.S. Army Air Corps also began ordering the plane about the same time.

Interchangeable fuselage nose sections were one feature of the plane. These enabled the A-20 to be used as either an attack bomber or strategic bomber.

When serving as an attack bomber, a nose section that housed four .30-caliber machine guns was installed. (These were in addition to the six other .30-caliber guns the plane carried.) When the plane's mission was to bomb a preselected target, it was fitted with a bombardment nose that contained bomb-aiming devices.

A handful of A-20s was loaned by the British

for the first all-American air strike against Hitler's "fortress Europe." It was considered appropriate that the attack be carried out on July 4 (1942).

German airfields in Holland were the target. It was a troubled mission. Two American planes were downed by antiaircraft fire and a flak burst tore away the propeller on the starboard engine of a third plane. When the engine caught fire along with the wing, the bomber quickly lost altitude, then slammed belly-first into the ground at the German base. The pilot, Capt. Charles C. Kegelman, bounced the plane back up into the sky, applied full power to his one good engine, and fled across the English Channel to make a safe landing at home. Kegelman won a Distinguished Flying Cross, the first awarded an American in Europe.

More A-20s were produced than any other attack bomber. Besides being used by the United States and its European allies, the Havoc saw duty with air forces of Brazil, the Netherlands, the Soviet Union, Canada, Australia, New Zealand, and South Africa. The 7,385th, and last, Havoc rolled off the production line on September 20, 1944.

Other Data (Model: A-20K)
Wingspan: 61 ft., 4 in.
Length: 48 ft., 4 in.
Power Plant: Two 1,700-hp Wright Cyclones
Loaded Weight: 27,000 lb.
Maximum Speed: 333 mph at 15,600 ft.

A formation of A-20s wing their way toward targets in continental Europe.

Twin-engine A-29 Hudson was designed as a commercial airliner, later converted to duty as a light bomber.

A-29 earned nickname of "Old Boomerang" for its ability to struggle back to its home base after being battered by enemy fire.

LOCKHEED A-29 HUDSON

Lockheed's A-29 Hudson was designed as a commercial airliner. A squat, twin-engine mid-wing monoplane, it was meant to carry fourteen passengers and a crew of four. It made its first flight on June 29, 1937.

The following year, with war threatening in Europe, the British Air Ministry ordered 250 A-29s for use as Royal Air Force bombers. More powerful engines were installed. Passenger seats were ripped out to make way for bomb storage and the bomb bay. A bombardier's position was built into the nose.

A pair of .30-caliber machine guns were mounted in the upper fuselage forward of the pilot, and a dorsal turret was added forward of the tail.

The first Hudsons to reach England were delivered by sea to Liverpool early in 1939. But after war broke out in September, 1939, production models of the plane were flown directly from the United States to British airfields.

Although it was originally designed for peaceful purposes, the Hudson achieved a number of notable "firsts" as a warplane. It was:

• The first RAF aircraft operated from England to destroy an enemy plane
• The first RAF aircraft to sink a submarine by rocket fire

• The first plane operated by the U.S. Army Air Force to sink a German submarine in World War II

A Hudson was also the first airplane in history to capture a submarine. In August, 1941, a Hudson bombed and strafed the *U-570* into submission, then circled the vessel until surface craft arrived to take the sub and its crew in tow.

Although not a fast plane and not particularly well armed, the Hudson had an excellent record for durability. Crew members sometimes referred to the ship as "Old Boomerang" because, although badly damaged by enemy fire, it always seemed to return from its missions. One Hudson managed to struggle back to its home base after having an engine destroyed, its fuselage ripped open, and its tail and both wings riddled with gunfire.

Well over 2,500 Hudsons were built. They saw service on every continent and many continued to play an active role right up until the war's end.

Other Data (Model: A-29)
Wingspan: 65 ft., 6 in.
Lenght: 44 ft., 3 in.
Power Plant: Two 1,200-hp Wright Cyclones
Loaded Weight: 20,500 lb.
Maximum Speed: 254 mph at 15,000 ft.

Lockheed turned out more than 2,500 Hudsons for service during World War II.

NORTH AMERICAN B-25 MITCHELL

On April 1, 1942, sixteen North American B-25 Mitchell bombers were hoisted aboard the aircraft carrier *Hornet* at Alameda, California, and parked on the open deck. The ship then headed out through the Golden Gate and into the open sea.

At the time, Americans needed some good news. Pearl Harbor was still a shambles. Wake Island and the Philippines had fallen to the Japanese.

The B-25s aboard the *Hornet* were meant to provide Americans with a boost in morale. Their mission was to attack Japan.

The planes had been readied for the raid by removing most of their guns and fitting the interior spaces with extra fuel tanks.

On the morning of April 17, the planes were ordered into the air. Each was armed with three 500-pound bombs and clusters of incendiaries. Despite heavy antiaircraft fire, the B-25s were successful in bombing Tokyo, Nagoya, Kobe, and Yokohama.

Since the planes did not have sufficient fuel for a return flight to the *Hornet*, they continued west to the mainland of China. A few crash-landed but in most cases crews bailed out, ditching the planes. Nine of the eighty Americans who took part in the raid died and all the aircraft were lost.

The attack jolted Japan's military leaders. From that day on, they were forced to hold fighters in

B-25 Mitchells aboard the aircraft carrier *Hornet* on the way to Japan for historic bombing raid.

reserve against the possibility of future attacks. And the daring raid raised the spirit of America at a time it needed raising.

Even before the historic strike, the B-25 Mitchell was the most popular of all two-engined bombers among American pilots. It was a great plane to fly, an "honest" plane. Later models offered an enormous amount of firepower—fourteen .50 caliber machine guns, plus, in the nose, a 75-mm cannon.

The B-25 was designed in 1938 and named for Gen. William "Billy" Mitchell, who had pleaded the cause of air power a decade before. The first production models were ordered in 1939. Eventually, a total of 9,816 B-25s were produced.

The B-25 was one of the most versatile of all aircraft. Not only was it used for high- and low-level bombing, but for ground strafing, photoreconnaissance, antisubmarine warfare, and even as a fighter. Mitchells were flown by the U.S. Army

Named for hero, Gen. William "Billy" Mitchell, B-25 was flown by Navy and Marine Corps pilots, as well as those of the Air Force.

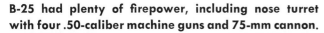

B-25 had plenty of firepower, including nose turret with four .50-caliber machine guns and 75-mm cannon.

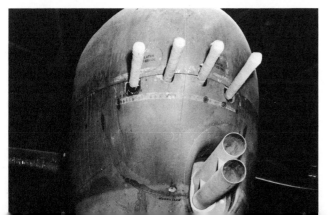

Air Corps, the Navy and Marines, and also by the English, Dutch, Chinese, Russians, and Australians.

Other Data (Model: B-25J)
Wingspan: 67 ft., 7 in.
Length: 52 ft., 11 in.
Power Plant: Two 1,700-hp Wright Cyclones
Loaded Weight: 35,000 lb.
Maximum Speed: 272 mph at 13,000 ft.

MARTIN B-26 MARAUDER

While North American's B-25 Mitchell was a favorite among pilots, the Martin B-26 Marauder was anything but. A "hot" and skittish plane, it took a very good crew to fly it. There were so many Marauder crashes in its early years that it was dubbed the "widow maker."

Once in combat, however, the Marauder lived down this reputation, compiling an outstanding record throughout Europe, in Africa and the Pacific. It had the lowest loss rate of any American aircraft.

When the B-26 was being tested in November, 1940, it was called the "Flying Torpedo" because of the smallness of the plane's wings in relation to the size of its body. Flight tests demonstrated that the Marauder was even faster than the Air Force had originally requested. It zipped along at 320 mph. It could also haul a heavier bomb load than had been specified—5,800 pounds.

B-26s went into action for the first time in April, 1942, in attack against Japanese positions at Port Moresby, New Guinea. Their speed and defensive firepower were a shock to Japanese fighter pilots. Two months later, B-26s were used as torpedo planes during the Battle of Midway.

When Marauders attacked an electrical generating plant at Ijmuiden, Holland, on May 14, 1943, it marked the plane's debut in Europe. More than 250 B-26s completed at least one hundred

B-26 Marauders fly in formation during Armed Forces Day festivities.

missions each. One B-26, nicknamed "Flak Bait," was the first Allied aircraft to complete two hundred missions.

After the invasion of Europe on June 6, 1944, B-26s, along with A-20 Havocs, concentrated on hitting targets that would most benefit the ground troops as they pushed toward Germany. The planes bombed bridges, highway junctions, gun positions, supply dumps, railroad yards, and airfields.

The low levels at which the aircraft flew made them especially vulnerable to antiaircraft fire, and they could be hit by lighter weapons as well. They sometimes suffered very heavy losses as a result.

In total, B-26s completed more than 110,000 missions, and they dropped more than 150,000 tons of bombs.

B-26s also saw action in Korea. Indeed, on July 27, 1953, the very day on which truce terms were finally agreed upon, B-26s roamed across North Korea, bombing and strafing targets as far north as the Yalu River.

Other Data (Model: B-26G)
Wingspan: 71 ft.
Length: 58 ft., 6 in.
Power Plant: Two 2,000-hp Pratt & Whitney
    Double Wasps
Loaded Weight: 37,000 lb.
Maximum Speed: 283 mph at 5,000 ft.

During test stages, B-26 was called "Flying Torpedo" because of its large body and relatively small wings.

BOEING B-29 SUPERFORTRESS

By mid-1944, the United States had been at war with Japan for two-and-one-half years. And except for the handful of B-25s that had attacked Tokyo and other cities in April, 1942, Japan had not felt the sting of American air power. Yet American military leaders realized that massive air bombardment was going to be needed to wreck the Japanese war machine.

The problem was one of distance. No bomber of the day had the range to fly to Japan from existing bases, drop its cargo, and return.

The Boeing B-29 Superfortress solved that problem. A four-engine aircraft, it could range 1,600 miles from its base, operate at high altitude, carry more than seven tons of bombs and, like the B-17 and B-24, fight off enemy planes. The B-29, more than any other weapon, brought about Japan's defeat and surrender.

On January 29, 1940, the Air Corps asked the Boeing Company to submit designs for a new, long-range heavy bomber, one superior to the B-17 and B-24. The first experimental model of the plane was ready for testing in September, 1941. Even before flight tests, however, the Air Force ordered 1,664 Superfortresses.

Some observers say that the Air Force rushed the B-29 into service too quickly. In some early planes, engine crankcases caught fire in the air

In both speed and range, B-29 Superfortress was far superior to B-17 Flying Fortress and B-24 Liberator.

and efforts to put them out were often in vain. Gun-sighting blisters exploded at high altitudes or frosted up so badly that gunners couldn't see through them. There were ignition system failures, too. But one by one, these problems were solved.

The B-29s started rolling off production lines in the autumn of 1943. It was decided that the plane could be used with greater effectiveness in the Pacific than in Europe.

At the time, however, China offered the only bases from which Japan could be reached. But China-based aircraft had to be flown over the Himalayan Mountains. Weather conditions were often brutal. These factors, combined with the plane's mechanical problems, limited the number of missions flown to about two a month per plane, not enough to bother the Japanese very much.

A turning point came when American forces captured the Mariana Islands in the summer of 1944. The B-29s that had been operating from China were switched to the Marianas, to Saipan, Tinian, and Guam, closer to Tokyo by 600 miles.

The first Superfortresses landed at Saipan's Isley Field on October 12, 1944. Tinian's airstrip began operation in December and Guam's in February, 1945.

Fleets of B-29s began attacking one Japanese city after another. The planes carried incendiaries, bombs filled with napalm to start fires.

On the night of March 9, 1945, some 334 aircraft set out to attack Tokyo in what was one of the most devastating raids of the war. The attack turned the city into a roaring inferno. It left 83,793 people dead and more than a million homeless.

The city of Nagoya was next, then Osaka and Kobe. American strategy was clear: to burn Japan out of the war.

Its four 2,200-hp Wright Cyclone engines enabled the B-29 to cruise at 364 mph.

On February 19, 1945, American marines launched an assault on Iwo Jima, a tiny island of black, volcanic ash, halfway between the Marianas and Japan. It was the bloodiest battle in Marine Corps history, costing 4,554 lives.

Once in American hands, Iwo provided landing fields on which crippled B-29s could set down

39

Smoke billows above Hiroshima following burst of first nuclear bomb.

after bombing Japan. These fields were also used by the P-51 fighter planes that escorted the bombers.

The B-29 attacks continued through the spring and summer of 1945. At the end, Japan lay helpless.

At 8:15 A.M. on August 6, 1945, a B-29 named *Enola Gay*, piloted by Col. Paul W. Tibbets, loosed a single bomb over the city of Hiroshima. Tibbets banked sharply after the drop, then leveled off to watch. He saw the enormous fireball and the towering mushroom cloud. War had entered the nuclear age.

On August 9, a second nuclear bomb was dropped on the port of Nagasaki. The Hiroshima bomb killed 78,000; in Nagasaki, casualties were only slightly less.

Negotiations for peace were underway. On August 14, 828 B-29s made their heaviest attack of the war. Not a single plane was lost in the raid. Before the last aircraft had touched down at its home base, President Harry Truman was able to announce Japan's surrender.

In the years just after World War II, the Strategic Air Command (SAC) was formed. Its mission was to be able to deliver anywhere at anytime enough destructive power to wipe out any nation. This capability was judged to be the strongest possible deterrent to war.

Improved B-29s were used as SAC's strike force.

The range of the Superfortress was increased to 5,000 miles. Crews were given advanced training in in-flight refueling, instrument flying, and radar-bombing techniques.

When war broke out in Korea in 1950, B-29s were thrown into battle. Their targets were railyards, steel plants, oil depots, and bridges. Superfortresses flew 1,076 days of the 1,126-day war, dropping 160,000 tons of bombs, only eleven tons less than B-29s had dropped on Japan during World War II.

By the end of the Korean War, the B-29 was obsolete, a propeller aircraft in the jet age, and due to be phased out in favor of the B-50. A total of 3,950 B-29s had been built.

Other Data (Model: B-29B)
Wingspan: 141 ft., 3 in.
Length: 99 ft.
Power Plant: Four 2,200-hp air-cooled Wright
    Cyclones
Loaded Weight: 137,500 lb.
Maximum Speed: 364 mph at 25,000 ft.

The *Enola Gay* lands at Mariana base after dropping nuclear bomb on Hiroshima.

DOUGLAS A-26 INVADER

Developed by the Douglas Aircraft Corporation as a follow-up to the successful A-20 Havoc, the A-26 Invader was the fastest and most versatile attack bomber of World War II. In 1944, an A-26 raced a De Havilland Mosquito, the speediest of all British attack bombers, for a distance of one thousand miles. The American plane finished the race twenty minutes ahead of its opponent.

As early as 1940, the Air Corps realized that its standard attack bombers—the A-20 Havoc, B-25 Mitchell, and B-26 Marauder—could be improved upon. Douglas began the design and development of three experimental models in 1941. These were the XA-26, a conventional attack bomber; the XA-26A, a version to be used as a night fighter; and the XA-26B, which was fitted with heavy armament and meant to be used as a gunship.

The XA-26, the bomber version, was ready for testing on July 10, 1942. Shortly after, it went into production.

Invaders first saw combat in 1944, striking targets in France. Not only was the Invader fast, boasting a maximum speed of 373 mph, it was a very rugged plane. In the first seventeen missions flown by A-26s, only one plane was lost. Time after time, A-26s would return from missions with only one engine operating.

A total of 2,446 A-26s has been built by the time the war ended in 1945. Contracts that called for the production of 4,500 more were cancelled.

That was not the end of the story, however. The Invader continued on active duty and in 1958 was redesignated the B-26 (although it had no relation to the Martin B-26 Marauder). Under its new designation, the plane won acclaim as a night bomber in Korea in the three years the war raged there.

Besides the usual problems of night intruder Missions, including antiaircraft fire, bad weather, and lack of visibility, Invader pilots had to contend with the treacherous Korean terrain. Mountains would rise abruptly from a flat plain to an altitude of 7,500 feet. Enemy soldiers sometimes stretched thick steel cables from one mountaintop to another, hoping to snag the tail or wing tip of a low-flying B-26. It worked more than a few times.

B-26s flew 53,000 sorties over Korea, four-fifths of them at night. They struck enemy troop concentrations, vehicles, rail lines, and airfields. After the Korean War, the B-26 saw service in Vietnam, also as a night bomber.

Other Data (Model: A-26C)
Wingspan: 70 ft.
Length: 51 ft., 3 in.
Power Plant: Two 2,000-hp Pratt & Whitney Wasps
Loaded Weight: 35,000 lb.
Maximum Speed: 373 mph

Douglas A-26 Invader was fastest and most versatile of all World War II attack bombers.

Futuristic-looking B-35 Flying Wing was one of most unusual bombers ever flown.

NORTHROP B-35 FLYING WING

One of the most unusual bombers ever flown, Northrop's B-35 was an attempt to design an airplane that was pure supporting surface—no fuselage, no tail surfaces, no exposed engine housing.

There were many advantages to a plane of such design. Every exposed portion of the aircraft contributed to the creation of upward pressure, to lift. Drag was decreased, since there was no fuselage or other drag-creating surfaces.

The B-35 dates to the early stages of World War II, when England seemed on the brink of being knocked out of the war. If that happened, a bomber would be needed capable of flying non-stop to Germany-occupied Europe, dropping its payload, and returning. The B-35 was proposed as a plane to meet that need.

Two B-35 prototypes were ordered by the Air Force in November, 1941. These were four-engine, propeller-driven aircraft. The propellers were the pusher type.

Serious problems were involved in designing the propellers, which had to be able to rotate in either direction, and the war ended before the first prototypes were completed. The XB-35 first flew on June 25, 1946.

By this time, the jet age had arrived. It was decided to convert the XB-35s to eight-engine jets. The new plane, designated the YB-49, made its

An experimental version of the B-35 being readied for testing at Hawthorne, California

first test flight on October 21, 1947. Air Force officials working on the project said the YB-49 was one of the ". . . most trouble-free and ready-to-fly bombers ever received from an Air Force contractor." It was called "a fine ship with a real future."

After more testing, thirty Flying Wings were ordered by the Air Force. But this order was later cancelled and the money used to buy B-36 Peacemakers.

The Air Force continued to keep the Flying Wing program alive until October, 1953, when the last of them was scrapped. Today, the only existing Flying Wing is to be found in a storage hangar maintained by the Northrop Corporation in Ontario, California.

Other Data (Model: XB-35)
Wingspan: 72 ft.
Length: 53 ft., 1 in.
Power Plant: Four 3,000-hp Pratt & Whitney
    Wasp Majors
Loaded Weight: 209,000 lb.
Maximum Speed: 391 mph

The B-36 Peacemaker, the "mightiest plane ever built"

CONVAIR B-36 PEACEMAKER

Hitler's war machine crushed Poland in 1939, then moved swiftly across the face of western Europe. Denmark, Norway, Belgium, Luxembourg, The Netherlands, and France fell to the Germans in a shocking three-month period in 1940. Great Britain loomed as the next victim.

In April, 1941, Air Force planners in the United States called for a bomber that would be able to strike European targets from bases in the United States should Britain fall. They wanted a plane that was capable of carrying a 10,000-pound payload a distance of 5,000 miles without refueling. They wanted it to be capable of flying at an altitude of 35,000 feet at speeds of 240 to 300 mph.

Of the four designs submitted by the aircraft industry, the Air Force chose Consolidated's Model 36. Consolidated, which was soon to become Consolidated-Vultee, and later Convair, was almost totally occupied with manufacturing B-24 Liberators at the time. Work on the XB-36, as it was called, was slow-paced. The first plane was not ready for testing until August 28, 1947. (World War II had been over for two years by that time.)

The B-36 was an enormous plane, its fuselage 2½ times longer than that of the Liberator. It had a swept-back wing that measured 230 feet from one tip to the other, and was 7½ feet thick at its deepest point.

The B-36 was called "the mightiest plane ever built"—and for good reason. Its ten jet engines generated a cruising speed of close to 400 mph, well beyond what the Air Force had originally asked for. It had a cruising range of 6,800 miles and could carry a bomb load of 86,000 pounds.

A total of 385 B-36s were delivered to the Air Force.

The B-36 never dropped a bomb in combat. But once, during a test run of the original XB-36, the plane did drop, by accident, a fifty-pound instrument for measuring air speed that it had dangled from a long cable. The missile tore through the roof of a Fort Worth, Texas, elementary school, scoring a direct hit on the boys' bathroom, hurting no one, but destroying a toilet.

Other Data (Model: B-36J)
Wingspan: 230 ft.
Length: 162 ft.
Power Plant: Six 3,800-hp air-cooled Pratt & Whitney Wasp Majors and four 5,200-lb.-thrust General Electric turbojets.
Loaded Weight: 410,000
Maximum Speed: 411 mph at 36,400 ft.

A total of 385 B-36s were produced at Convair's Fort Worth plant.

During the late 1940s and early 1950s, the B-47 served with the Strategic Air Command in every corner of the globe.

BOEING B-47 STRATOJET

The six-engine B-47 Stratojet achieved several notable firsts. It was the first Air Force bomber to be designed "from the ground up" and it was the world's first swept-wing jet to be ordered in quantity. More than 2,000 were built. It was also the first bomber in the world to be capable of exceeding 600 mph in level flight.

The B-47 was operated by a three-man crew— a pilot, copilot, and a "three-headed monster," a man who had three jobs, that of navigator, bombardier, and radar operator.

Boeing began developing the B-47 in 1943. The basic design underwent constant revising. One of the changes called for swept-back wings, which permitted a significant increase in the plane's speed. Although heavier than the heaviest bomber of World War II, the B-47 was classified as a medium bomber by the Air Force.

Two experimental B-47s were built by the Boeing Company in Seattle, Washington. The first of these flew in December, 1947. After extensive testing, ten B-47As were ordered in November, 1948. Major production then began.

More design changes followed, however. One version of the plane, the XB-47D, had two prop-jet engines turning four-bladed engines and two turbojet engines. This design was meant to give the plane greater range. It was never put into production, however.

B-47 Stratojet was world's first swept-wing jet to be mass-produced.

The fifth and final model of the Stratojet, the B-47E, had a longer fuselage and more powerful engines than its predecessors. Thirty-three booster rockets helped to get it into the air on takeoffs.

The plane had a maximum speed of more than 600 mph at 16,300 feet. Its range was 4,000 miles. However, the plane had intercontinental striking power, thanks to air-to-air refueling. One B-47E traveled 39,200 miles nonstop in 80 hours, 36 minutes.

During the late 1940s and much of the 1950s, the B-47 was the mainstay of the Strategic Air Command, and was spotted at SAC bases in every corner of the world. The Stratojet was eventually phased out in favor of the B-52.

Other Data (Model: B-47E)
Wingspan: 116 ft.
Length: 106 ft., 8 in.
Power Plant: Six 6,000-lb.-thrust General Electric
    J-47 turbojets.
Loaded Weight: 200,000 lb.
Maximum Speed: 640 mph

The B-50 Superfortress became quickly obsolete, a victim of the jet age.

BOEING B-50 SUPERFORTRESS

The B-50 was the first bomber built for the Strategic Air Command after World War II. A propeller plane, it soon, like the B-29, became obsolete, a victim of the jet age.

It was no coincidence that the B-50 was very similar in appearance to the B-29, for it was developed directly from that plane. In 1944, a B-29A was fitted with four 3,500-horsepower Pratt & Whitney Wasp Major engines (in place of the original 2,200-horsepower Wright Cyclones), equipped with taller fin and rudder, lighter but stronger wing sections, and a newly designed undercarriage.

Vastly improved performance was the result. Sixty of these planes were ordered as B-29Ds, but their designation was changed to B-50s before delivery began.

Manned by a crew of six, which included two refueling operations, the B-50 could travel at 380 mph at 25,000 feet. Its cruising speed was 277 mph.

The plane carried two .50-caliber machine guns in each of three remotely controlled turrets, four .50s in a front turret, and two .50s and a 20-mm cannon in a tail turret. It also carried a 20,000-pound bombload.

In 1949, a B-50A, the *Lucky Lady II*, made aviation history by completing the first nonstop flight around the world. During its 23,452-mile journey, which began and ended in Fort Worth, Texas, the *Lucky Lady II* was refueled four times —over the Azores, Saudi Arabia, the Philippines, and the Hawaiian Islands. The plane spent 94 hours, one minute in the air and traveled at an average speed of 294 mph.

In a later version of the B-50, two jet engines were added under the plane's wings to increase

Developed directly from the B-29, the B-50 was very similar in appearance to that plane.

speed. While this alteration may have postponed the plane's retirement, it could not prevent it.

The last B-50s to be built were completed in 1952. But these were used, not as strategic bombers, but to train crews for the huge Convair B-36. Designated as TB-50Hs, these were the largest training planes ever built.

Other B-50s that were unwanted as bombers once jet aircraft became available were converted for use as KB-50 aerial tankers—flying gas stations.

KB-50s were widely used by the Air Force during the late 1950s.

Other Data (Model: B-50)
Wingspan: 141 ft., 3 in.
Length: 99 ft.
Power Plant: Four 3,500-hp Pratt & Whitney
    Wasp Majors
Loaded Weight: 173,000 lb.
Maximum Speed: 380 mph at 25,000 ft.

No bomber has served the Air Force longer than the B-52 Stratofortress.

BOEING B-52 STRATOFORTRESS

A striking plane with swept-back wings and a tall, clipped tail, the Boeing B-52 gave the United States a truly all-jet intercontinental strategic air arm. The plane served as the standard Air Force bomber through the 1960s and 1970s and into the 1980s.

The B-52 had some unusual design features. Its eight Pratt & Whitney J-57 turbojets were carried in paired pods beneath the wings. The plane's four-unit landing gear could swivel to the right or left, allowing the aircraft to face directly into the wind on crosswind landings while still rolling straight down the runway. This helped to prevent the plane from drifting to one side or the other as it taxied.

The B-52 began life in 1946 when Boeing was awarded a contract to produce designs for a straight-wing, long-range bomber to be powered by six turboprop engines. By October, 1948, the designs had undergone many changes. The first prototype, built as Model 464, flew on April 15, 1952.

The first B-52A did not make its appearance until 1954. Only three B-52As were built, and all were used for further testing and development. They were followed by 34 C models and 170 D models.

These early B-52s were responsible for some amazing feats. In November, 1956, eight Stratofortresses completed record nonstop flights of 17,000 miles on routes that carried them over the North Pole. One of these planes was in the air for 31½ hours (thanks, of course, to aerial refueling).

The following year, three B-52s flew around the world in 45 hours, 19 minutes, a record. They averaged 530 mph over the 24,325 miles.

And in August, 1956, a B-52G completed a 28-hour, 12,942 mile nonstop flight that took it over every state capital in the continental United States, including Juneau, Alaska.

The first B-52H came off the production line on September 30, 1960, and made its first flight the following March. The H model was capable of flying halfway around the world—12,500 miles—without refueling.

The 744th, and last, Stratofortress—a B-52H—came off the assembly line at Boeing's Wichita, Kansas, plant on June 22, 1962.

When the United States was drawn into the war in Vietnam in the mid-1960s, Stratofortresses were given several roles to play. But they were often roles unlike any that had been planned for the

In-flight refueling enabled the B-52 to make record nonstop flights.

aircraft, which was originally intended to put whole cities and industrial complexes under attack.

For instance, when clusters of enemy troops were discovered in jungle hideouts, B-52s were sometimes brought in from Anderson Air Force Base in Guam, 2,530 miles away, to bomb the area where the soldiers had been spotted. B-52s also struck a variety of other targets in North and

A Strategic Air Command B-52 drops a load of bombs during mission over Vietnam.

South Vietnam, in the DMZ (the demilitarized zone between the North and the South), and in Laos and Cambodia.

During eleven days in December, 1972, B-52s, despite fierce antiaircraft fire, which included sophisticated Soviet SAM (surface-to-air) missiles, pounded strategic targets in the Hanoi-Haiphong area in Vietnam's north from their bases in Guam.

It marked the first time these targets had been touched during the war.

The U.S. Air Force remembers the period as the "Eleven Day War." In that space of time, the B-52s dropped more than 49,000 bombs on airfields and other military targets. Fifteen B-52s were lost during the action, all victims of SAMs.

Many observers believe the bombing led to a

resumption of peace talks, which had been broken off by the North Vietnamese. On January 27, 1973, the peace pacts were finally signed.

The B-52 received a new lease on life in the late 1970s, thanks to the development of the cruise missile. Once launched, a cruise missile can accurately steer itself to a distant target. A B-52 can carry three jet-powered, nuclear-armed weapons in racks beneath its wings in rotary launchers in the weapons bay.

Late model B-52s were also armed with the Hound Dog ASMs (air-to-surface missiles) and AGMs (air-to-ground missiles) or AGM-6A SRAMs (short range attack missiles). In addition, the plane could carry a 70,000-pound bombload.

In the mid-1980s, the B-52 was still being judged as an effective—although somewhat tired—weapons system. It had earned the distinction of having served longer than any other bomber in history.

Other Data (Model: B-52H)
Wingspan: 185 ft.
Length: 157 ft., 7 in.
Power Plant: Eight 17,000-lb.-thrust Pratt
   & Whitney turbojets
Loaded Weight: 505,000 lb.
Maximum Speed: 630 mph at over 24,000 ft.

B-52 carried eight Pratt & Whitney turbojet engines in paired pods beneath its wings.

B-58 Hustler was world's first supersonic bomber.

56

CONVAIR B-58 HUSTLER

Convair's B-58 Hustler, first flown on November 11, 1956, was the world's first supersonic bomber. It blazed along at 1,385 mph at 40,000 feet, which was faster than most fighter planes of the day.

From the day the first model was rolled out for Air Force officials and media representatives, the B-58 was a sensation. It was the first bomber with a sleek delta wing, a triangular surface that served as both the wing and horizontal stabilizer.

The Hustler also featured a disposable pod beneath the fuselage. Design engineers felt it made no sense for a bomber to include storage space for bombs that had been dropped or fuel that had been consumed. So they designed the Hustler without any bomb bay or tanks for extra fuel. The pod carried the nuclear or conventional bombload and a portion of the aircraft's fuel. When the pod was empty, the pilot dropped it. In addition to the bomb and fuel pod, the B-58 could be fitted with a pod containing electronic surveillance equipment.

The B-58 was highly accurate as a bomber, thanks to the advanced navigation and weapons system with which it was equipped. But speed is what the plane became famous for. During the ten years the B-58 was flown by the Air Force, the plane established nineteen speed and altitude records.

A Hustler flew from New York to Paris in three hours, nineteen minutes, an average speed of 1,089 mph. Another flew from New York to Los Angeles in two hours, an average speed of 1,214 mph. And a third made the flight from Tokyo to London in eight hours, thirty-five minutes, an average speed of 939 mph. These records were recognized with international trophies.

Air Force test pilots said that the B-58 was never flown at its maximum speed for fear that its wings and body would begin to melt from the high temperatures produced by friction as the craft streaked through the sky.

The B-58 entered active service in March, 1960. It was not on active duty very long, however, for its role was taken over by intercontinental ballistics missiles, which were much less costly. B-58s were retired from service in 1969 and 1970.

Other Data (Model: B-58A)
Wingspan: 56 ft., 10 in.
Length: 96 ft., 9 in.
Power Plant: Four 10,000-lb.-thrust General
  Electric turbojets
Loaded Weight: Over 160,000 lb.
Maximum Speed: 1,385 mph at 40,000 feet.

B-58s move down production line at Fort Worth, Texas, plant.

The Air Force wants the B-1 to be America's No. 1 bomber of the 1990s.

ROCKWELL INTERNATIONAL B-1

The B-1, a four-engine, swing-wing supersonic aircraft, was developed to penetrate enemy airspace at treetop level and drop conventional or nuclear bombs or launch cruise missiles. One day it may be America's No. 1 bomber.

Sleek and menacing-looking, the B-1 carries a crew of four and holds eight cruise missiles, 12 to 24 nuclear bombs, or 64,000 pounds of conventional bombs. It has a top speed of almost 750 mph and can travel about 7,500 miles without refueling.

Slightly more than 150 feet long, the B-1 has wings mounted on pivots that tuck closely to the fuselage during high-altitude, high-speed flight. The wings extend outward, increasing lift during takeoffs, landings, and flight at low speeds.

The B-1 had its beginnings in November, 1969, when the Department of Defense requested design proposals for a bomber to take the place of the B-52. Contracts to build the airframe were awarded Rockwell International. General Electric was assigned to develop the plane's turbofan engine.

The B-1 made its first flight in December, 1974. Even before that, however, the plane was the center of heated debate. Critics of the big plane charged that it wasn't really needed, that its mis-

A B-1B gets refueled from a KC-135 tanker.

sion could be accomplished by land- and sea-launched nuclear missiles.

They also claimed that new kinds of air defenses had made conventional bombers obsolete. During the late 1970s, development work had begun on radar-evading planes, known as Advanced Technology bombers, or "stealth" bombers. Those who questioned the value of the B-1 said it would be better to put the money into Stealth aircraft.

The plane's cost also triggered criticism. Each B-1 cost an estimated $100 million, making it the most expensive combat aircraft ever built.

In 1977, President Jimmy Carter cancelled plans to produce the B-1, although he allowed some research and flight-testing to continue. After President Ronald Reagan was elected in 1980, he revived the B-1 program. He and his military advisers considered the B-1, along with the MX missile and Trident submarine, to be vital to the nation's defense. The President announced that the Air Force would receive one hundred B-1s.

From 1970, when development work on the B-1 began, to 1980, Rockwell International produced four B-1A models. The company then used

A B-1B takes off on test flight at Edwards Air Force Base in California.

these planes for testing in working to improve the B-1's design. This research and development program resulted in the B-1B, introduced late in 1984.

One of the biggest differences between the B-1A and B-1B was one of weight. The B-1B weighed about 477,000 pounds at takeoff, while the original plane weighed 395,000 pounds. The increase was a result of greater fuel capacity and the installation of heavy equipment necessary for launching cruise missiles.

Perhaps the most important change concerned the plane's "radar image." Improved electronic devices reduced the size of the image, giving the B-1B a "stealth" quality. Officials of Rockwell International said the B-1B's image, as viewed by enemy radar, would be only 10 percent as strong as the B-1A and only 1 percent as strong as the B-52.

The B-1B was only about two-thirds as large as the B-52. The plane could carry a weapon payload at least a third larger than the B-52. The B-1B was also about 60 percent faster.

Critics of the B-1 program were not any more enthusiastic about the B-1B than they were about the original plane. But when President Reagan was re-elected in 1984, it seemed to assure that the B-1 production schedule, which called for the completion of four planes per month beginning in 1985, would be met, and the Air Force would have its one hundred B-1 bombers by mid-1988.

Other Data (Model: B-1B)
Wingspan: Swept-back, 78 ft., 2.5 in.
    Extended, 136 ft., 8.5 in.
Length: 150 ft., 2.5 in.
Power Plant: Four 30,000-lb.-thrust General
    Electric F101-102 turbofans
Loaded Weight: 447,000
Maximum Speed: 1,320 mph at high altitude

Greater fuel capacity and missile-launching equipment make the B-1B a much heavier plane than earlier models.

Low-slung Stealth bomber may bear a resemblance to this artist's concept of a futuristic aircraft, its fuselage dwarfed by its wing.

STEALTH BOMBER

A magazine editor visiting the Air Force Office of Public Affairs in Washington was being shown color slides of present-day aircraft by a young lieutenant. One after another, views of such planes as the B-52 and B-1 bombers and the F-15 and F-16 fighters, popped onto the screen.

"Now, here's our latest weapon," the lieutenant said.

The screen went blank. After a few puzzled moments the editor said, "I don't see anything."

"That's right," the lieutenant replied with a grin. "The plane's invisible."

The plane the lieutenant was referring to was the Stealth bomber, an aircraft that would be virtually invisible to enemy detection devices. The Stealth may be the Air Force's No. 1 bomber in the 1990s and beyond.

The Air Force, incidentally, does not particularly like the word "stealth," which means furtive or sneaking. It prefers to call the project the ATB, short for Advanced Technology Bomber.

To elude enemy radar, the plane has many unique features:

Size: The smaller the plane is in cross section—the surface actually seen by radar—the less chance it has of being detected. The B-52 with its huge body and towering vertical stabilizer, is a cinch for radar to spot. The Stealth is squat and low-slung, almost like a Frisbee or flounder (or the B-35 Flying Wing, described earlier).

Shape: Sharp edges and abrupt angles, such as those produced by engine pods, give off strong radar echoes. The Stealth is completely streamlined. Its fuselage and cockpit are included in the wing. Its engines are built into the body.

Materials: The Stealth is not made of metal, or at least metal is eliminated wherever possible. Instead, materials that deflect or absorb radar waves will be used, chiefly carbon and fiberglass mixtures. The aircraft is to be covered in a fibre-reinforced graphite skin.

Such advances won't render the ATB entirely invisible to radar. There will still be a speck on the screen.

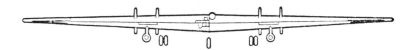

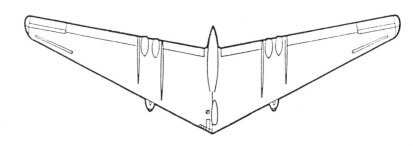

Stealth bomber will have characteristics of B-35 and YB-49 Flying Wings—no fuselage, no tail surfaces, and no exposed engine surfaces.

To eliminate that last tiny signal, the Stealth will carry new electronic gear that locates the radar station and then sends out the right signal to erase even the tiniest speck from the scope.

The overall effect is to put a blindfold over the radar's all-seeing eye. The first time the enemy will realize that the Stealth is on the attack is when the plane appears overhead and is visible to the naked eye.

AIRCRAFT OF THE NATIONAL AIR AND SPACE MUSEUM

The Wright Brothers' Military Flyer, the North American B-25 Mitchell, and the Boeing B-29 Superfortress—these and many of the other famous aircraft described in this book (and other books of the series) can be seen, studied, and photographed at facilities operated by the National Air and Space Museum in Washington, D.C.

Famous bombers and other aircraft can also be seen at several other museums in various parts of the country, but probably none equals the National Air and Space Museum in terms of exhibit quality and diversity. A part of the Smithsonian Institution, it claims to be Washington's most popular tourist attraction and the world's most popular museum of any kind.

The huge buildings that make up the museum stretch three city blocks and offer spectacular exhibits that represent the evolution of flight and space technology. Museum galleries are devoted to fourteen different themes, including World War I Military Aircraft, World War II Military Aircraft, Air-Sea Operations, and Jet Aircraft.

The museum also offers two theaters, where films related to flight are shown, and a research library and photographic collection. Free tours of the museum are offered daily.

Other of the museum's historically significant aircraft are to be found at the Paul E. Garber Preservation, Restoration, and Storage Facility located in Suitland, Maryland, not far from downtown Washington.

On exhibit in this "no frills" setting are approximately one hundred aircraft, as well as a number of spacecraft, engines, propellers, and other flight-related objects. Trained guides conduct free tours, including a behind-the-scenes look at a restoration workshop where aircraft and other objects are being preserved. Reservations to visit the Garber museum must be made in advance.

The facility was named for Paul E. Garber, a noted historian who joined the Smithsonian Institution in 1920, and was responsible for acquiring a large portion of the Smithsonian's Aeronautical Collection.

For more information about the National Air and Space Museum, write the Visitor Information Center, Smithsonian Institution, Washington, D.C. 20560.